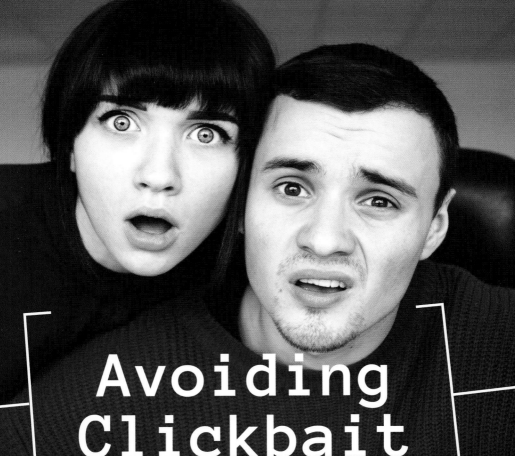

Avoiding Clickbait

Kristin Thiel

Cavendish Square

New York

Published in 2019 by Cavendish Square Publishing, LLC
243 5th Avenue, Suite 136, New York, NY 10016

Library of Congress Cataloging-in-Publication Data

Names: Thiel, Kristin.
Title: Avoiding clickbait / Kristin Thiel.
Description: New York : Cavendish Square, 2019. | Series:
News literacy | Includes glossary and index.
Identifiers: ISBN 9781502640208 (pbk.) | ISBN 9781502640215
(library bound) | ISBN 9781502640222 (ebook)
Subjects: LCSH: Internet--Juvenile literature. | World Wide Web--
Juvenile literature. | Computer fraud--Juvenile literature.
Classification: LCC TK5105.875.I57 T475 2019 | DDC 004.67'8--dc23

Editorial Director: David McNamara
Editor: Caitlyn Miller
Copy Editor: Lisa Goldstein
Associate Art Director: Alan Sliwinski
Designer: Joe Parenteau
Production Coordinator: Karol Szymczuk
Photo Research: J8 Media

The photographs in this book are used by permission and through the courtesy
of: Cover Bodnar Taras/Shutterstock.com; p. 4 Monkey Business Images/
Shutterstock.com; p. 6 Library of Congress/Corbis/VCG/Getty Images; p.8
ZUMA Press/Alamy Stock Photo; p. 11 NetPhotos/Alamy Stock Photo; p. 14 Pat
Greenhouse/The Boston Globe/Getty Images; p. 17 Castleski/Shutterstock.com;
p. 18 Artgraphixel/Shutterstock.com; P. 20, 32, 38, 40, 48, 49, 51 ScreenShots;
p. 21 James Hager/Robert Harding/Alamy Stock Photo; p. 23 Bettmann/Getty Images;
p. 24 Courtesy Lars Eidnes; p. 25 METOKARA/Wikimedia Commons/File:Veles,
Macedonia (FYROM) panoramio(20).jpg/CC BY SA 3.0; p. 26 Mandel Ngan/AFP/
Getty Images; p. 28 Cliparea l Custom media/Shutterstock.com; p. 31 Consuelo
Bautists/El Pais Photos/Newscom; p. 33 Grigorita Ko/Shutterstock.com; p. 37
Julie Alissi/J8 Media; p. 42 Dmytro Gilitukha/Shutterstock.com; p. 45 Ostill/iStock.
com; p. 46 Wrangler/Shutterstock.com; p. 52 Loskutniko/Shutterstock.com.

Printed in the United States of America

CONTENTS

Chapter 1.. 5
What Is Clickbait?

Chapter 2..15
Characteristics of Clickbait

Chapter 3..29
Resisting Clickbait

Chapter 4..47
Putting Your Skills into Action

Glossary 56

Further Information 57

Bibliography..59

Index...62

About the Author...64

Students use technology every day. That's why it's important to separate high-quality online content from content that is designed to get people to click on it, without offering any useful information.

What Is Clickbait?

Clickbait is a headline, image, or social media post that baits (or lures) people to click through to an article or video. Sometimes that article or video is also referred to as clickbait. Technology experts have said clickbait misrepresents what it will deliver to its audience. Its headline promises amazing or useful information. However, the story turns out to be uninteresting, false, or about a completely different topic.

There's also a different reason why some media experts believe certain websites publish clickbait. These sites don't mislead readers, but they do take advantage of readers' curiosity gaps. A curiosity gap is the space between what you know and what you need or want to know. Clickbait may try to fill that hole. Appealing to someone's curiosity sounds like a good thing. Yet these sites lure people in by appealing to their curiosity about unimportant matters.

Though experts argue about the exact definition of clickbait, there is no doubt that it has a hold on us. There are real reasons, often economic, why clickbait exists. There is also real science, based on brain research, why people both love and hate clickbait. This research helps us understand why people keep clicking on it. Fortunately, there are also ways to spot clickbait's telltale markers— and avoid it.

The Technique Behind Clickbait

The word "clickbait" is an invention of the internet age. However, the marketing technique of overpromising and underdelivering is an old one. It is also a diverse tactic. Examples of overpromising appear in everything from circuses to late-night television shows.

Clickbait Techniques in Entertainment
The traveling circuses of the early twentieth century promised acts that were "the greatest" of this and

The Ringling Brothers circus billed itself as having the "world's greatest shows."

WHY DO PEOPLE HATE CLICKBAIT?

In 2015, the *New York Times* asked several media experts to discuss why clickbait has a bad reputation. After all, clickbait has been around for a long time. Nearly everyone knows it exists, and no one has ever put a stop to it.

Jazmine Hughes was one of the experts who weighed in with an answer about why clickbait feels wrong. Hughes had a serious problem with the way clickbait headlines shape readers' emotions. She said:

> The promise that "you won't believe what comes next" or "you'll never feel the same" ... [is] aggressive, empty and intellectually reductive—or, simply, super annoying.

Hughes said that the language used in clickbait shows that clickbait publishers do not trust their audience to know what to read. The audience is told what they will and will not believe and feel about a story. They are not expected to think about the information themselves. They do not even get a chance to read the information before they are told to react. Clickbait tells the audience their feelings right away, in the headline. To tell someone else how or what to feel is forward and aggressive, Hughes says. She also states that it is "intellectually reductive," or too simple to tell the kinds of complicated stories that people think deeply about. These are just a few of the key reasons that many people dislike clickbait.

the "most amazing" of that. Not every show could have the greatest horseback rider or the most amazing magician, however. Most acts were probably just okay, maybe good. The creators of the shows did not care about being honest. They needed to get paying customers in the door.

Infomercials were the "clickbait" of the late twentieth century. The expansion of television in the 1980s meant that more people than ever watched TV. In turn, this led networks, cable channels, and advertisers to make new attempts to grab customer dollars. Network and cable channels started to operate twenty-four hours a day. This opened new ad slots. Companies billing products as "too good to be true" ran infomercials in the middle

Pitchmen like Billy Mays (*center*) made infomercials a popular form of advertising.

of the night. Infomercials' technique was nothing new. They overpromised and often underdelivered. These thirty- or sixty-minute television "programs" were actually long commercials.

Clickbait Techniques in Print Journalism

In the 1800s, yellow journalism was the name for sensational or exaggerated storytelling. It was dangerous because it was published as news in newspapers. Really, these stories were meant to attract people and encourage them to buy copies of the newspapers. Their focus was not on careful or important reporting. In the early 1900s, William Randolph Hearst's *New York Journal* was in stiff competition with Joseph Pulitzer's *New York World*. Both newspapers ran wildly exciting headlines that often distorted the truth or lied. At least one 1913 front page of the *World* included a "Skirmish!" box to show how much bigger its circulation was than its rivals'.

In journalism's more recent history, Vinnie Musetto became the "godfather of clickbait," as the *New Yorker* called him. He wrote headlines for the *New York Post* in the 1980s that baited readers into buying copies of the newspaper. One of Musetto's most famous headlines promised a big story about a particularly scary murder. However, the article did not focus on the clever, eye-catching details in Musetto's headline. Also, the reported-on event happened at a small bar in a distant part of New York City. It was not the sort of story that normally would make the front page of a big-city newspaper. However, Musetto's irresistible headline made it front-page news.

CLICKBAIT FOR
THE PAYCHECK

In 2017, Snopes, a website that researches rumors and urban legends, studied clickbait coming from verified celebrity Facebook pages. Celebrities sending clickbait to their audiences may be a type of so-called influencer marketing. Influencer marketing is big business for both companies and people who have influence in society, like celebrities. People trust celebrities or want to be like them. That means people are more likely to buy certain products if celebrities say they use those products. In exchange for recommending a product, a celebrity receives the product for free or is paid by the company making the product. Under Federal Trade Commission (FTC) regulation, celebrities must tell people that they are being paid to recommend the product.

There is no regulation regarding the clickbait that Snopes tracked. Facebook users following certain celebrities received posts from those celebrities in their Facebook news feeds. These posts directed readers to click on links to articles with sensational headlines. Viewers clicked on those links, believing the celebrities they trusted wanted to share important news with them. Instead, they were taken to sites full of fake news, ads, and ad trackers.

Snopes reached out to the celebrities as well as the agencies they employed to put content on their Facebook

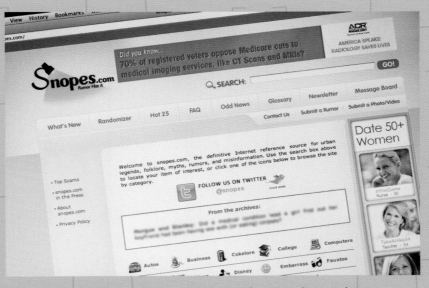

Snopes is a website known for trying to determine whether rumors are true or not. In 2017, Snopes examined clickbait posted by celebrities.

accounts. Those who replied said they had no idea how the clickbait got on the celebrities' pages. No one was admitting to posting clickbait on purpose—or getting paid to do so. This might be a case of celebrities, or the people who manage their business, being dishonest. On the other hand, the celebrities themselves could be victims of hacking. Perhaps without the celebrities' permission or even knowledge, the clickbait sites posted information from those celebrity accounts. Either way, this is just one way that clickbait spreads.

"Contagious Media"

Viral content is online content that is shared over and over. Clickbait is a type of viral content. The idea of "going viral" has been around since people started using the internet with some regularity, in the late 1990s. Web designer Jonah Peretti told National Public Radio that he could think of examples of people clicking and sharing web content as far back as 1996. He called this the "bored-at-work network." Not wanting to work, people sitting in their offices looked at funny or surprising things on the internet and in their email. In May 2005, Peretti and his employer, Eyebeam, a media arts organization, held the Contagious Media Showdown. They wanted to see how far and fast someone could get a bit of information or entertainment to spread via the internet.

It was the first major mainstream acknowledgment of "clickbait." (That said, people had been experimenting for years before that with trying to get content to travel from person to person across the internet.) Two days after the contest launched, the *Huffington Post* started. The site "pioneered" what would soon be called clickbait, public media outlet KQED says. Its "content seemed to take control of the mind, causing the hand almost involuntarily to click on whatever was there." A year and a half later, in December 2006, a web development expert named Jay Geiger defined "clickbait" in a blog post.

Clickbait: The Big Picture

Clickbait can be harmless. Think about when a person clicks to view a photo of a cute kitten and nothing happens except that person sees a photo of a cute kitten. However, sometimes it can cause big problems. Clickbait sometimes spreads quickly, even if it offers false information. Its purpose may not be to inform but to get readers to buy something or to give away their personal data. If it is any or all those things, there can be harmful consequences. These consequences include customers wasting hard-earned money and people's personal information being sold to companies that misuse this data. That's why it's important to think before you click.

The Ice Bucket Challenge went viral in 2014. Some viral stories are considered clickbait, but not all clickbait is bad.

Characteristics of Clickbait

Clickbait has been around a long time, in one form or another. The term "clickbait" also means different things to different people. If clickbait as a whole can come in many forms, we need to look more closely at its parts. Knowing the parts of clickbait is an essential way of learning to avoid the negative clickbait. It is also important to understand where clickbait comes from, how it spreads, and why people are likely to continue creating it.

Clickbait Stories Can Be Viral Stories

A viral story is one that has spread far and wide. If a lot of people have seen a piece of online content in a short amount of time, it has "gone viral." Just because an article or picture gets a lot of clicks does not mean it will go viral. To go viral, a story usually needs to be shared person to person, just like a virus's germs need to be shared. Any story that receives a lot of clicks usually becomes more visible in search engines and social media feeds. That means the more people that click, the greater the chance clickbait has at going viral. People often believe a story matters if it is highly visible or if they know many others have shared it. But stories with a lot of "shares" aren't always important or filled with good information. Look at viral stories with a critical eye. Decide for yourself if they are the negative kind of clickbait.

Fake News Can Be Clickbait

Fake news is a deliberately fabricated, falsified story that has been made to look like truthful news. Clickbait articles are not necessarily fake news. Clickbait may be misleading but offer information that is technically true. However, fake news is often clickbait because the people behind the fake news want lots of people to click on it.

Spot the Bait

There are many indicators of clickbait. These indicators include the need to click through several pages and over-the-top headlines.

Multiple Clicks Required

If you click on a headline and then must click through several pages before you get to the point of the story, you

Fake news is never breaking news. It just makes false information look like real news to get people to click.

may have read a clickbait article. For example, consider the Snopes study on celebrity Facebook accounts and clickbait. That study found that after people clicked the link in the Facebook post, they were not sent immediately to the promised article. Instead, they were directed to what is called a landing page containing only the story's image and headline. That page featured yet another link to click. If people clicked on that link, they were swept into a website full of ads, ad tracking software, and clickbait. It's possible they never saw the article they wanted to see in the first place.

BEHIND THE BUSINESS OF MEDIA: PAGE VIEWS

Publishers and producers of online content use clickbait because clickbait leads to page views. Page views lead to advertisements. Ads lead to revenue, or money, for media outlets.

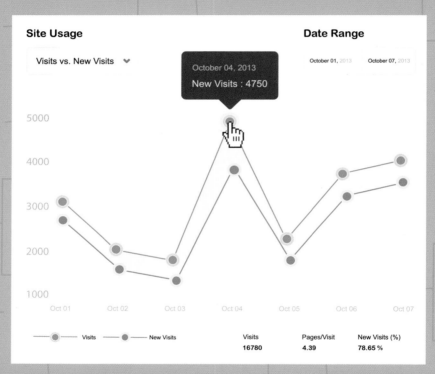

Site Usage

Visits vs. New Visits ⌄

October 04, 2013
New Visits : 4750

Date Range

October 01, 2013   October 07, 2013

5000

4000

3000

2000

1000

Oct 01   Oct 02   Oct 03   Oct 04   Oct 05   Oct 06   Oct 07

● Visits   ● New Visits

Visits	Pages/Visit	New Visits (%)
16780	4.39	78.65 %

Analysts study how many people visit websites and view the pages using dashboards like this one.

A business chooses where to advertise based on how many potential customers will see that ad. This means a media outlet needs to prove how many people view its content. It may do this by measuring the number of page views it receives. A lot of page views may equal a large audience. Clickbait content often requires little effort to create but delivers a lot of click-throughs, which equal a large number of page views. Publishing clickbait can seem like an easy way to increase audience size—and possibly earn more advertising money.

Search engines and social media complicate matters for publishers seeking page views. There is so much information on the internet that Google, Facebook, and other sites cannot show people everything that is available at any one time. They use algorithms to determine what to offer. For example, Facebook considers around one hundred thousand factors, personal to each user, to determine what to show a person when they refresh their Facebook news feed. If a link does not meet enough of those criteria, it does not appear for that person. These algorithms change often. Google tweaks its algorithm hundreds of times a year. Some of those revisions are major enough to affect whether a link is shown or not. Media outlets are always trying to determine the best ways to catch an audience. The people that run search engines and social media say this can lower the amount of clickbait. Yet sometimes this means the creation of clickbait worded differently enough to slip past the algorithm.

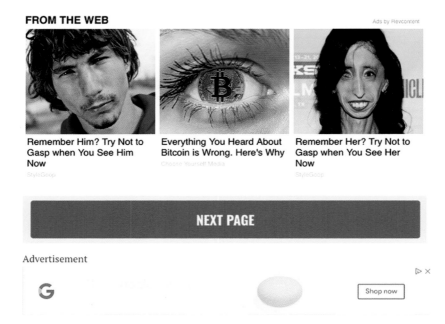

Attention-grabbing photos and captions indicate that these stories link to clickbait.

You may also see this multiclick technique in articles that rely on lists. For example, consider an article titled something like "Is Your Best Friend Talking About You Behind Your Back? She Is, If She Does One of These Five Things." The article may deliver on those five things. However, each reason will be on its own page. This requires the reader to click several times to read the whole article.

Wild Headlines

Clickbait announces itself right away: with its headline. By reading article titles critically, carefully, and thoughtfully, you may avoid clicking. Headline language that sounds

The *New York Times* published a story about birds called pin-tailed whydahs (*right*). Some critics said the headline seemed like clickbait.

like a rumor may be clickbait. If a headline starts with the phrase "You won't believe" or "What happened next will shock you," the story may be clickbait. The language makes the reader curious. This curiosity inspires an urge to click the headline to learn the unbelievable or shocking answer.

It can be difficult to tell from a headline whether an article or video is an example of negative clickbait. It's tricky to determine because legitimate news stories also have engaging headlines. Even the *New York Times* has been accused of publishing clickbait. Some readers have been bothered by *Times* headlines like "This Beautiful Parasitic Bird Could Soon Turn Up in Your Yard." The newspaper responded to these complaints by saying that "the job of a headline is to get people to read the article in a manner that is true to the story."

An attention-grabbing headline is acceptable to the *Times* as long as it does *not* do two things. First, a good headline does not mislead the audience. Second, the article will live up to the headline's promise. A good headline also does not say so much that the audience thinks they can read only the headline and know the full story.

For fun, the *Independent* wrote a short history of the world in clickbait headlines. Here are a few of them:

- "This Man Thought He Was Going to India. What He Found Next Will Astonish You" (Christopher Columbus's voyage)
- "Two Bicycle Repairmen in Kitty Hawk Will Change The Way You Think About Travel" (the Wright brothers' first airplane flight)
- "When These Men Stepped Inside This Capsule, They Were In Houston. You'll Never Guess Where They Stepped Out" (the first moon landing)

Interesting headlines are not necessarily bad. Real, verifiable news also uses well-written headlines to encourage people to read. The difference is that clickbait usually makes claims that cannot really be confirmed, demonstrated, or proved. Clickbait headlines sound desperate. A real news headline sounds like it wants to give you information. Alternatively, a clickbait headline sounds like it wants you to click—right now.

Why Clickbait Is Here to Stay

New advertising technology is starting to push clickbait aside. It is no longer worthwhile to many American-based businesses to seek payment by the click. However, if the world market has any say, clickbait will not fully disappear from consumers' view. Businesses based in other

Written a certain way, even real news, like Orville
Wright flying, can appear to be clickbait.

countries still see more money when American audiences
click on their articles.

BuzzFeed News wrote that the US 2016 presidential
election was "a digital gold rush" for people in Veles, a
small town in Macedonia (a country in Eastern Europe).
During the election, at least 140 websites publishing
stories about American politics came out of Veles.
These sites had American-sounding, and legitimate-
sounding, web addresses such as WorldPoliticus.com,
TrumpVision365.com, USConservativeToday.com,
USADailyPolitics.com, and DonaldTrumpNews.co. They
did not publish truthful stories. They published over-
the-top stories that encouraged people to click to read
one outrageous claim after another. (Note that last URL,

ARTIFICIAL INTELLIGENCE AND CLICKBAIT

Some computers are capable of learning in a way similar to how humans learn. These computers use data to understand new data on their own and to learn from their mistakes. This technology is being used for all sorts of practical applications, including writing clickbait headlines.

Lars Eidnes, a Norwegian software developer, created software that generates such headlines. He wrote on his blog in 2015 that he has been surprised how successful his creation has been: "Most of them [the headlines] are grammatically correct, and a lot of them even *make sense*."

Lars Eidnes created software that writes clickbait headlines.

It helps, Eidnes wrote, that many clickbait headlines are generic. One example he listed was *BuzzFeed*'s 2015 article "50 Disney Channel Original Movies, Ranked by Feminism." A computer using Eidnes's software would not have to know anything about current events or real people to create a headline like that. It would just need to know keywords a website's users are interested in, like "movies" and "feminism," as well as some grammar.

From there, with self-learning, computers using Eidnes's software can add specifics to the headlines. Eidnes's computer learned how to include names in a headline. Then it learned which words were popular names. It may not know who a celebrity is or even if he or she is in the news, but it correctly guesses to use the name anyway.

During the 2016 US presidential election, Veles, Macedonia, was the home of many websites that published fake news about American politics.

DonaldTrumpNews.co. If you looked at it quickly, you might not notice that it ends with ".co" and not ".com." An unusual URL like that is an indication that the site you are visiting may not provide legitimate information.)

The people behind the sites did not care who won the American election. They cared about the money they could earn by creating such sites. Most people in Macedonia do not make a lot of money. Teenagers in particular do not make much money because they are not supposed to work. This unique way to make money on the internet allowed even young people to profit. One teenager said that he made $16,000 between August and November 2016 from ads on his two websites. The average salary in Macedonia for that time period was $1,484.

Businesses that churn out clickbait have been labeled clickbait farms, clickbait factories, or clickbait

Clickbait farms discovered that it was profitable to publish fake news in support of Donald Trump during the 2016 presidential election.

complexes. Whatever you call them, these businesses are not powered just by young people in remote locations. In October 2014, the content on Israel's PlayBuzz became some of the most shared on Facebook around the world. PlayBuzz had the second-most shared content worldwide. The only site with content shared more on Facebook was the *Huffington Post*.

The Macedonians making money with clickbait also focused on Facebook. They learned they could generate a lot of traffic if their stories spread on Facebook. Over-the-top content in support of Donald Trump was the most successfully spread. Therefore, they created a lot of false information designed to delight Trump supporters. "Yes, the info in the blogs is bad, false, and misleading," one Veles university student who ran one of these sites told *BuzzFeed News*. It was more important to him to get clicks than to spread truthful information. He and other clickbait farms found stories from elsewhere on the web, gave them new, attention-grabbing headlines, and republished them. The website owners spent most of their effort not on reporting but on getting others to share stories across social media. Each click led to more money from ads on their websites.

To a savvy internet user, the stories from Macedonian clickbait farms are obviously clickbait. Smart readers know to look out for wild headlines and stories that require a reader to click many times to reach the content that interests them.

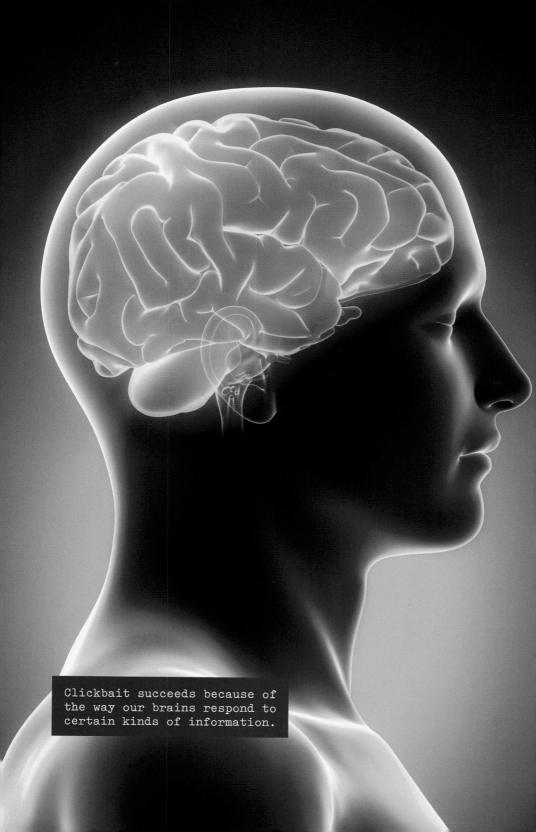

Clickbait succeeds because of the way our brains respond to certain kinds of information.

Resisting
Clickbait

The best way to resist clickbait is to first understand it. It's critical to know why it works so well and what some of its components are. According to experts, clickbait works because it manipulates our emotions and our brains' organizational skills. Our feelings and the way our brains organize information are hugely important in our daily lives. Clickbait publishers prey on how our minds work. Luckily, you can learn some specific steps to take so that you do not fall for the lure.

Some of the Science Behind Why Clickbait Works

Emotional Manipulation

People who write clickbait headlines know that the more emotional they make those headlines, the more likely people are to click on them. This has foundation in biology, says Jonah Berger, who studies social influence at the University of Pennsylvania. Humans often make decisions based on emotions as much as reason—if not more so. Berger told *Wired* that these emotional instincts are what "clickbait headlines rely on."

Researchers out of Brazil and Qatar shared data about this idea in a report. "Breaking the News: First Impressions Matter on Online News" studied 69,907 headlines from four international media outlets. The researchers concluded that headlines "influence one's mindset" to an extreme degree. Even if a reader finishes an entire article, he or she will recall only details that match what they were expecting based on the headline. Furthermore, the most read articles are the ones that have the most extreme headlines. In short, we are most likely to click on a headline that affects us emotionally. We are most likely to remember only what we felt from that headline even after reading the whole article.

Gap Fulfillment

Clickbait is known to stir up curiosity with its headlines and to promise to deliver answers sure to delight or horrify. Clickbait's appeal to our curiosity works also because of what makes us human. In the 1990s, George Loewenstein, an economist and a psychologist, proposed the information-gap theory. It says that people have an emotional response when they realize they do not know something they want to know. People have an even stronger response when they know just a little about the

George Loewenstein studies human behavior, including information-gap theory.

information they know they are lacking. When presented with a clickbait headline that promises to fill an information gap, a person may click.

Mental Organization

Listicles, articles written mostly or completely as lists, are popular clickbait forms. This is because they help readers organize and understand information. Here, clickbait again uses human's characteristics to its advantage.

Numbers, which most listicles use, stand out in a sea of words on websites. Since they are different from everything that surrounds them, they can grab readers' attention. They also organize information spatially, meaning they position the information carefully on the page. Our brains do well with spatial learning.

If a headline promises "11 Reasons" or "8 Steps" or "Something New in Less than 30 Minutes," people may be more encouraged to click. They know they will receive all the information the article has to offer quickly. They know what to expect, an estimate of how much time they need to spend, and that there will be a satisfying end. At least, that is what they are promised.

This article uses a list to encourage people to click.

Numbers also promise that we do not have to choose. The article "11 Reasons Why …" will present readers with eleven reasons. The article will contain not an unknown number of reasons that the reader will have to rank in his or her mind. Lists, *Wired* explained, "help create an easier reading (and thinking) experience."

Cats, Goats, and the Next Cute Animal

All those cute or funny animal pictures that circulate can also be considered clickbait. They draw people in and encourage them to click to see more. Animal photos present an interesting case, however. Unlike a lot of other negative clickbait, a clickbait headline promising photos of cute animals usually delivers on that promise.

(It is possible that an animal photo will be tied to ads, more clickbait, or other negative sites, content, or data-gathering software, so these photos are not always innocent forms of clickbait.)

Humans love cute photos in part because they delight our brains at the chemical level. Seeing something cute gives us the same chemical rush that eating sugar does. That rush is from a chemical in our brains called dopamine. It helps us feel good and happy. This alone is interesting when we think about why clickbait works. But there is even more fascinating science to this story.

Stanford biology and neurology professor Robert Sapolsky has explained dopamine and motivation through an experiment. The experiment involved a light, a lever, some food, and a monkey. The monkey learned that when

Cute animal photos can be clickbait too.

a light in the lab turned on (this is called the signal), he could press a lever (the work that needs to be done), and then he would receive food (the reward for doing the work). Interestingly, the monkey's dopamine levels rose not when he received the food but when the light turned on. The promise of the reward gave the monkey more joy than receiving the reward. It turns out, Sapolsky said, that "dopamine is not about pleasure; it's about the anticipation of pleasure. It's about the pursuit of happiness rather than happiness itself."

Here is how anticipation works in relation to animal-photo clickbait: the headline signals the brain that something cute is coming. We do the work by clicking to see that cuteness. Then we are rewarded with the cuteness. The signal, the headline, is more crucial to the release of dopamine than the reward (the photo). "That effectively means the headline itself is what gave you pleasure—not for what it was, mind you, but for what it represented," *Wired* explained.

That is not all. Sapolsky explained that researchers then adjusted the experiment with the monkey. Now, the monkey received a food reward only half of the times the light signal came on and he worked the lever. The monkey did not lose interest or grow frustrated or sad. Instead, every time the signal came on, the monkey's dopamine levels skyrocketed. The word "maybe," Sapolsky said, "is addictive like nothing else out there." Knowing he *might* be rewarded led to more happiness for the monkey than knowing he would be rewarded for sure.

SOCIAL MEDIA VS. CLICKBAIT

Clickbait gets attention, and social media sites like Facebook run on attention. That's why clickbait started showing up higher in people's Facebook news feeds. In 2014, many users started telling Facebook they did not like those types of headlines. These users preferred stories from friends and trusted news sources in their feeds. Since then, Facebook has been trying to weed out clickbait.

In 2016, Facebook explained that it identified tens of thousands of headlines as clickbait. To identify clickbait, Facebook asked two questions of each headline. The first question was, Does it withhold information, forcing people who want to know what the article is about to click? The second question was, Does it exaggerate the article, promising more than the article offers?

This data helped Facebook build a system to spot commonly used phrases in clickbait. The Facebook system is similar to how a filter weeds spam out of email inboxes. Clickbait was then posted in a lower spot in Facebook news feeds, moving clickbait more out of view. In 2017, Facebook improved its process to spot more clickbait and post it even farther down in news feeds.

This demonstrates why some people repeatedly fall for clickbait, even when they have recognized the signs and know something is clickbait. Humans, like monkeys, are willing to be disappointed a lot of the time—if we are not disappointed some of the time. Cue the cute animals or other satisfying content. They provide that clickbait reward often enough that people keep clicking on other kinds of clickbait articles. Wondering "Will I be rewarded this time, or will I not be?" is powerful. People end up craving a chance to ask that question. Clickbait is nothing but the pursuit of happiness, so no wonder it works so well!

Sapolsky noted that if you block the dopamine from happening in the brain, a human (or a monkey) will not attempt the work. It does not matter how frequently the reward is offered. Behind the monkey experiment is the power of dopamine. Clickbait's control over our dopamine is in its headline, its signal. If there were not such enticing headlines, there may be no clickbait.

More Ways to Spot the Bait

AdEspresso helps businesses create successful Facebook ads. Its post on how to create clickbait that is successful on Facebook can help internet users avoid clickbait. The details AdEspresso thinks are good are what readers should be aware of when reading information online.

Specificity

Clickbait headlines may feel generic a lot of the time, but they are not all the time. AdEspresso applauded a post from a smartwatch company that mentioned exactly how many people had backed its Kickstarter fundraising campaign, exactly how much money was left to be raised in exactly how many days, and what percentage of savings people who clicked could receive. These very specific numbers indicate to readers that there's "something interesting or irresistible that people can't afford to miss." The deadline to sign on for savings is "urgency-creating." The information in this clickbait may be true, exaggerated, or false. Whatever it is, you are likely to believe it is worth your click. However, just because there are details does not mean they make sense or matter to you.

Images

Many websites know their users' locations. If an article is using your location to try to get you to click, it may be clickbait. As an example, AdEspresso shared a realtor ad. The ad's image was personalized to show the viewer's

home city. Because the map looks familiar, you may feel more comfortable clicking. Robocalls, or automated calls, from

Sites use your location to tailor their articles to catch your attention.

telemarketers are doing something similar. Neighbor spoofing is when a robocall appears to come from a phone number with your same area code and first three digits. The familiarity is attention grabbing. That makes it difficult to resist answering. You think it is someone you know because you recognize six of the ten digits in the phone number. That's the same with a tailored clickbait image. Your brain thinks this content knows you and knows what you need.

Images connected with clickbait can also be altered to appear more interesting. If an image does not look like it was taken for the story that is being presented, that may be clickbait. A reverse image search may help you figure out if the photo is naturally connected to the story, before you click. A reverse image search is when you search using an image you've found. This helps to identify the source of the image. Google offers an easy way to search using an image, as do other internet companies.

"Reverse search" the images in articles to learn if they are real or really connected to that article.

Truncated Ads

AdEspresso shared a piece that stood out as clickbait because its headline was cut off. What the viewer saw was "Cow Is So Terrified Of Going To Slaughter She Starts To Cry. Now W." A legitimate news source will never let its audience wonder what word starts with "W." If a site does not look professionally made, it may contain content that does not want to give you information. Instead, it wants your clicks.

Native Advertising

Clickbait is based on a page-view economic model. Publishers use clickbait because it leads to page views, which can lead to more money from more advertising. However, this standard is changing.

Clickbait came into being at a time when the number of clicks on an article was a key way to measure success. That is why clickbait headlines were often sensational and unconnected to their articles. Publishers did not care what happened after the click because their money came from the click. Just as clickbait manipulates human emotions, humans, guided by emotion, started turning against clickbait. Being misled made people angry and want to take action.

Native advertising is an alternative to page views. Native ad campaigns succeed not if a person clicks but if a person stays and engages with the content. Native advertising looks like editorial content or like your friend's post on social media. However, it is paid for or sponsored. (Native advertising should always have a label saying it is paid content.) Native ads fit in with the other content a user is reviewing. Studies have found that the longer people spend with content, the more it pays off for companies. Users who spend a long time reading a native ad are more likely to return to that site or consider the associated company when it was time to buy that product.

Successful native ad pieces include certain information. Their headlines ask "how" or "why" questions and use emotional and descriptive language. Their images are unique yet make sense with the written content. Native ads are truthful but not boring. They entertain, even using humor. Above all, they are "honest and authentic—in other words, human," *Adweek* explained.

Native ads sound a lot like clickbait. They may be "less annoying" than clickbait, as the *New York Times* has said. Nonetheless, audiences should be aware of them and be careful not to confuse them with content written from legitimate news sources.

Instagram

Success Story

Building Awareness for the Levi's® Lifestyle

The classic American retailer used Instagram to style its apparel as the uniform for living in the moment, reaching 7.4 million people. In addition, 24% of people who saw more than one ad remembered seeing a Levi's® ad.

7.4M	24-pt
people in the U.S. were reached	lift in ad recall, an increase of nearly 3x over the control group

Some ads appear like real news stories or friends' social media accounts. Levi's ran a native ad that reached millions of people.

Identify and Resist Clickbait

To resist clickbait, understand that you hold the power. Remember that everyone wants your clicks. It is up to you to determine what sites should get them. Be skeptical. Ask questions. Do not read just one source and believe it immediately.

Ask the right experts too. This can be trickier than it sounds. If you read a story about your school principal getting a new puppy and you want to confirm that that story is correct, you can easily guess who to ask. Your English teacher, your coach, and your grandfather are all experts in their own ways. However, it is unlikely that any of them can confirm the existence of your principal's new buddy. Instead, you should ask your principal.

Science News for Students offered a more difficult example of confirming a story. How do you confirm the details of a forest fire? Firefighters, fire investigators, and government officials are all good possible experts on this. Of course, they still may not know how the fire started for sure. If they were not there, they can only piece together the clues and make an educated guess.

Research the writers of the articles you read and the websites that publish their stories. Anyone can publish on the internet. That's why it is important to know if someone has been trained as a journalist and if the website checks its writers' facts. Try to find out if the writer or website has a bias. Sometimes sites are sponsored by businesses or advocacy groups that expect all articles to present ideas they agree with.

Major events like forest fires can, and should, be fact-checked by readers.

Remember that it may mean something if you cannot easily fact-check an article. Usually, reporters want to name their sources and link to the research papers they cite. If the sources are anonymous and the facts are vague, you should wonder what that means about the story's truth.

MediaShift has suggested people give each piece of information they find online the SMELL Test. Readers should think about a piece's Source, Motivation, Evidence, and Logic, as well as what is Left out of the piece. The first letters of those words spell "SMELL."

Source

Ask yourself, who wrote the piece and published it, and who was quoted in the piece?

You can often find writer biographies online. Click on the author's name, and you may be taken to more information. You can also type the writer's name into a search engine. Ideally, a writer has formal training or other published stories. That means that person has had the opportunity to learn how to write a credible story. If there are links to other published stories, check those to see how many of those are clickbait articles. If the writer has a history of writing such content, the story you are considering reading may also be clickbait.

You can also find out about the publication itself online. Sites that are full of ads and have oddly formatted headlines (such as with all caps) are likely full of clickbait. There is usually a link to an About page in a menu along the top of the website or in a list at the bottom. Some sites will state clearly that they are humor sites that offer funny—but false—information. You may also want to then search for the publication's name elsewhere online. Learn what other people say about it. A publication's About page may make it sound well-established and unbiased, but other credible sites may help explain the publication's bias or respectability.

Sources should be named, not anonymous. Sometimes a story is so sensitive that the identities of people interviewed must be kept secret for their safety. Most times, first and last names can be included, as well as job titles. People who were involved in the event are usually more credible than people who heard about the event from someone else. Think also about the source's expertise. Do they have a lot of experience or education in the subject the journalist is asking them about?

Motivation

Even the most trustworthy journalists and sources have bias—all humans do. If someone involved in a piece online wants to sell something, promote something, or support something, that person may choose to include only certain details. These selected details might encourage readers to think like the writer does. Some people's main goal with a story is to inform you, so you can make your own decisions. Some people want to persuade you, so you follow their lead. There are ways to spot a piece that is doing more informing than persuading. Every fact is backed up with a credible source. Multiple sides of an issue are presented evenly. There is no judgment about what happened or who was involved. Readers are not asked to act on the information.

Just as all writers have bias, so do all readers. We are attracted to articles that support the way we already think. Sometimes you need to consider your own motivation too. If an article makes a point of confirming what you already believe, it may be clickbait.

Evidence

Even if you trust everything about the story after taking it through the "S" and the "M" of "SMELL," you want to continue to the "E." Do your own investigation. A lot of things in most stories have been said elsewhere online too. Search for a claim or quote and see if you can find other sources that confirm it. Watch out that other mentions are not just copies of the article you are looking at. You are searching for different mentions of the same idea.

Investigate, question, and draw your own informed conclusions about everything on the internet.

Logic

Does the story make sense? Simply put, use and trust your own brain. You can connect the dots too. Here are some things you can think about: Are the quotes just anecdotes, or personal examples, that the writer is making sound bigger than they are? Is other content over the top? Do the details in a piece support the point or conclusion? Just because a writer presents quotes and facts as relevant does not mean they are. Always read critically.

Left Out

What does a piece not say about its topic or sources? MediaShift suggested searching elsewhere online for other sources on a topic, "especially those that differ by gender, generation, geography, race or class." A story can be accurate and incomplete.

Clickbait that you want to avoid is often misleading, incomplete, or incorrect. Become a savvier, smarter consumer of online content. You will waste less of your time on clickbait—and learn and share more valuable, useful information.

The internet is a powerful tool, so you must use your critical thinking skills when you're online.

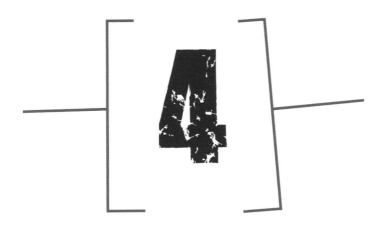

Putting Your Skills into Action

Researchers at the Stanford Graduate School of Education found that "otherwise digital-savvy students can easily be duped" by information online. Middle school, high school, and college students are experts at using computers, smart technology, and the internet. However, they still struggle with knowing what is an ad and what is a legitimate news story.

The researchers asked students to separate legitimate sources from unreliable ones and explain why. In one example, middle schoolers were shown an article on financial planning. The students were also told that a bank executive wrote the article. A bank paid to have it written and published. The students did not question the bias of the writer. Even if the information provided was true, it was likely only one side of the story. Both the author and the sponsor had reasons—such as job security—for sharing information that benefited or promoted their personal perspective.

In another example, students were asked to look at the home page of the website *Slate*. This time, they could separate news stories and traditional ads. Those ads had a lot of clear markers that set them apart from journalism, such as being in a text box or offering a coupon code. However, most students did not notice or understand the label "sponsored content" that indicates something is a native ad. More than 80 percent of the middle school students surveyed thought paid content was legitimate news.

If the term "sponsored content" is on a piece, it is an ad. This article is labeled "sponsored content" in the upper-left corner.

A CLICKBAIT ODYSSEY

Odyssey is a website that was started by two college seniors.

I n 2010, college seniors Evan Burns and Adrian France started a newspaper for sororities and fraternities. Four years later, Burns had digitized the paper and widened its scope. Most of its writers continued to be college students. But the content was now for everyone, not just sororities and fraternities. As of 2017, investors had given the site (now renamed Odyssey) $32 million. As important, the site's articles were averaging thirty million views a month—people kept clicking on the content.

The site is both clickbait and community. A site does not have to be one or the other, and that is one of the reasons that clickbait can be so difficult to spot.

"9 Out of 10 Americans Are Completely Wrong About This Mind-Blowing Fact"

As discussed, there are many forms of clickbait. At its most basic level, clickbait is anything you cannot resist clicking on. It may be useless, or it may be legitimate information. Either way, it has lured, or baited, you into giving it your attention, or clicking on it.

At its most innocent, clickbait may give you real, useful information. An article on a sports team winning the championship after decades of being in last place, a comprehensive article on how a war started, or a profile that presents multiple perspectives on a world leader's actions may all receive a lot of clicks. Those examples are genuinely important or exciting—and they may also be true.

Clickbait may also be harmless but not useful—think, photos of cute kittens. However, clickbait can also be dangerous. News that is misleading or downright false can be clickbait. Even seemingly safe things like images of cute animals can be problematic. By clicking, you may be opening yourself up to viruses or ad tracker software. You may get pulled into a series of sites full of ads and other questionable pieces.

On March 3, 2013, almost exactly one year after the website *Upworthy* launched, the piece "9 Out of 10 Americans Are Completely Wrong About This Mind-Blowing Fact" received 1.57 million views or, in essence, clicks. Let's walk through how you would know if this is clickbait.

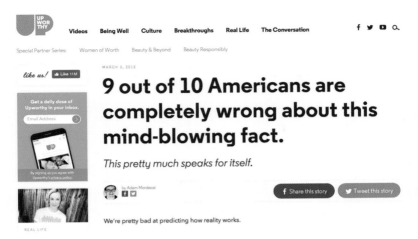

Videos   Being Well   Culture   Breakthroughs   Real Life   The Conversation

Special Partner Series: Women of Worth   Beauty & Beyond   Beauty Responsibly

MARCH 2, 2015

like us!   Like 11M

Get a daily dose of Upworthy in your inbox.

Email Address

By signing up you agree with Upworthy's privacy policy.

9 out of 10 Americans are completely wrong about this mind-blowing fact.

This pretty much speaks for itself.

by Adam Mordecai

Share this story   Tweet this story

We're pretty bad at predicting how reality works.

REAL LIFE

An article's headline, publisher, and author can help you determine if it is clickbait.

Headline

The headline is likely the first thing that caught your attention. A well-written, catchy title is not necessarily a bad thing. But this one may indicate clickbait for a couple of reasons. The specificity of "9 out of 10" tries to show that it is a researched article. To some, that headline comes across sounding like a commercial. What really points to clickbait are the phrases "completely wrong" and "mind-blowing." This is exaggerated language that cannot be proved true or false. These phrases also tug on readers' emotions. Some people's responses may be prideful: "Well, I am not one of the 9 out of 10 who are wrong!" Others may react out of fear: "Am I one of the 9 out of 10 who don't know this?" Others still might get excited: "I would like to learn something that will blow my mind on this boring day!"

Finally, the headline offers to fill a curiosity gap. Readers might wonder if they are one of the nine but also what fascinating fact we will learn by clicking. The piece has a subtitle, "This Pretty Much Speaks for Itself." That does not provide information. It does feed curiosity.

Content

Now move on to the content. There is a video at the top of the piece. One line of text introduces it: "We're pretty bad at predicting how reality works." Even after the "article" has started, the audience still knows nothing about what the piece is about. The freeze frame of the video shows an outline of the continental United States and a chart of percentages and stick-figure people. Readers do not know what those numbers are referring to. If you look carefully, you can see the words "Wealth Inequality in America."

Wealth inequality is real, but news about it may be presented as clickbait.

The text after the video gives the author's reaction to different moments during the video: "At 1:05, I get a rude awakening. At 1:41, he starts talking about you."

Once we watch the video, we realize the headline is misleading. The video is about wealth distribution in the United States—how many people have how much money. It talks about what the reality is, what people think the reality is, and what people wish the reality was. From the headline, we would think nine out of ten people do not know how wealth is actually distributed in the United States. That is the only fact that the headline could be referring to. However, the video never says how many people do not know that fact. Rather, the statistic of nine out of ten people refers to how many people want a certain ideal distribution of wealth.

Beyond the headline, some of the content is misleading. There is supposed to be a "bad" word at minute 2:24, according to the article. Because the author put quotation marks around the word "bad," we know he probably does not mean it's a swear word. Indeed, it is the word "socialist," a word that describes an economic system. In a society like the United States, many people do consider "socialist" a "bad" word. However, that is an opinion, not a fact. The article tricks us by previewing the word in that manner.

Viewers are also never directly told who produced or narrated the video. There is a list of references at the end of the video. If we paused the video and looked up each citation, we could fact-check what is said in the video and maybe make some assumptions about the bias of the people behind the video. At the very bottom of the article is a citation about where the video originated. Clicking on those links is an important way of checking who is responsible for the video.

In fact, clicking on the author's name takes us to his biography. In this example, the author's biography points to his social media feeds. It also says he is an editor-at-large at *Upworthy*, the very website on which his article is published.

It is up to you to consider all of these facts. Again, remember that clickbait is not always harmful. However, clickbait does use certain techniques to hook readers. Think carefully about the headline, the content, and the author. Decide for yourself if you think this video is an example of clickbait. Then, decide if you think it is an example of harmless clickbait or the kind that can have consequences.

Fighting Clickbait

From listicles to fake news, cuddly cat photos to misleading celebrity stories, lots of content online can be considered clickbait. If you feel almost powerless to resist clicking to read or see more, you have taken the bait. Brain science says it is natural and understandable that we fall for this style of content. However, we can override our emotions—a big motivator for clicking—and choose not to fall for clickbait. After all, it is often misleading, time-wasting, and problem-causing content. By stopping to think critically, we can easily identify clickbait and avoid it.

"THE VIROLOGIST"

In 2015, when the *New Yorker* wrote about him, Emerson Spartz was twenty-seven years old. He was already successful on the internet. His first website, which he built when he was twelve, became the most popular *Harry Potter* fan site in the world. With the money he made from that, he started Spartz, Inc. The company builds and launches websites, all of which have one goal: to make viral content. That can be considered clickbait: if an article or video is spreading far and wide, like a virus, it has baited people to click on it.

Spartz told the *New Yorker* that when he was a kid, he read biographies of people successful at their jobs. What he learned inspired him to do this work. "I realized that influence was [directly] linked to impact—the more influence you had, the more impact you could create." Beyond influence and impact, creating viral content is a superpower, Spartz believes. He explained: "I realized that if you could make ideas go viral, you could tip elections, start movements, revolutionize industries." In other words, Spartz knows the true power of the internet. He is saying he knows online content can shape people's ideas and opinions.

Spartz's success is a good reminder that the people behind viral content have many goals. Some want to make money. Others want to change the world. Many want to do both. Always think through the motivation behind the content you read.

GLOSSARY

ad tracking A method to check how many clicks something receives.

algorithm A procedure for accomplishing something, especially by a computer.

bias A personal prejudice.

fabricate Invent, make up, usually in order to trick people.

fake news Propaganda, deliberate misinformation.

landing page Usually, a website's home page.

native advertising Online content that looks like the publication's editorial content but is paid for by an advertiser.

page view An instance or visit to a particular page on a website. Higher page views can allow website publishers to charge more money for ads on their sites. This is because more people will look at the ads.

sensational Using exciting, wild details to cause intense curiosity or emotional reaction.

skeptical The quality of asking questions about what you read, instead of automatically believing it.

source A person who supplies information.

verifiable Able to be confirmed as real.

FURTHER INFORMATION

Books

Dell, Pamela. *Understanding Social Media.* Cracking the Media Literacy Code. North Mankato, MN: Capstone Press, 2018.

Harris, Duchess, and Laura K. Murray. *Uncovering Bias in the News.* News Literacy. North Mankato, MN: Core Library, 2018.

Websites

Factitious

http://factitious.augamestudio.com/#

Play a free online game to test your ability to tell fake news from real news.

Real vs. Fake News: How to Avoid Lies, Hoaxes, and Clickbait and Find the Truth

http://library.sbcc.edu/findsearch/research-guides/real-vs-fake-news-how-to-avoid-lies-hoaxes-and-clickbait-and-find-the-truth/#tabs-15516-0-1

Learn more about understanding and evaluating online information.

Videos

Fake News' Impact on Politics

https://www.youtube.com/watch?v=1jfCZHGJyiw

CBS News provides details about clickbait's effect on the 2016 presidential election.

How False News Can Spread

https://ed.ted.com/lessons/how-false-news-can-spread-noah-tavlin

Educator Noah Tavlin explains how to look for misleading or fake news, while discussing how false information spreads.

What Makes Something Go Viral?

http://bigthink.com/videos/what-makes-something -go-viral

Professor Scott Galloway describes how online content goes viral.

BIBLIOGRAPHY

Beaujon, Andrew. "The Real Problem with Clickbait." Poynter, July 16, 2014. https://www.poynter.org/news/real-problem-clickbait.

Cassidy, John. "The Godfather of Clickbait." *New Yorker*, June 10, 2015. https://www.newyorker.com/news/john-cassidy/the-godfather-of-clickbait.

Donald, Brooke. "Stanford Researchers Find Students Have Trouble Judging the Credibility of Information Online." Stanford Graduate School of Education News Center, November 22, 2016. https://ed.stanford.edu/news/stanford-researchers-find-students-have-trouble-judging-credibility-information-online.

Eidnes, Lars. "Auto-Generating Clickbait with Recurrent Neural Networks." Lars Eidnes' Blog, October 13, 2015. https://larseidnes.com/2015/10/13/auto-generating-clickbait-with-recurrent-neural-networks.

Gallagher, Sean. "You Won't Believe Why Facebook Will Block This Headline." *Ars Technica*, May 18, 2017. https://arstechnica.com/information-technology/2017/05/facebook-adjusts-algorithm-will-bury-articles-with-clickbait-headlines.

Gardiner, Bryan. "You'll Be Outraged at How Easy It Was to Get You to Click on This Headline." *Wired*,

December 18, 2015. https://www.wired.com/2015/12/psychology-of-clickbait.

LaFrance, Adrienne, and Robinson Meyer. "Famous Headlines, Rewritten for Facebook's New Clickbait Policy." *Atlantic*, August 4, 2016. https://www.theatlantic.com/technology/archive/2016/08/famous-headlines-rewritten-to-comply-with-facebooks-new-policy/494603.

Manjoo, Farhad. "Fall of the Banner Ad: The Monster That Swallowed the Web." *New York Times*, November 5, 2014. https://www.nytimes.com/2014/11/06/technology/personaltech/banner-ads-the-monsters-that-swallowed-the-web.html.

Marantz, Andrew. "The Virologist." *New Yorker*, January 5, 2015. https://www.newyorker.com/magazine/2015/01/05/virologist.

McManus, John. "Don't Be Fooled: Use the SMELL Test to Separate Fact from Fiction Online." MediaShift, February 7, 2013. http://mediashift.org/2013/02/dont-be-fooled-use-the-smell-test-to-separate-fact-from-fiction-online038.

Meyer, Robinson. "Why Are Upworthy Headlines Suddenly Everywhere?" *Atlantic*, December 8, 2013. https://www.theatlantic.com/technology/archive/2013/12/why-are-upworthy-headlines-suddenly-everywhere/282048.

New York Times. "How We Define Clickbait (Which We Do Our Best to Avoid)." July 21, 2017. https://www.nytimes.com/2017/07/21/reader-center/clickbait.html.

Petri, Alexandra. "A History of the World in Clickbait Headlines." *Independent*, June 5, 2015. http://www. independent.co.uk/news/media/a-history-of-the-world-in-clickbait-headlines-10300783.html.

Peysakhovich, Alex, and Kristin Hendrix. "News Feed FYI: Further Reducing Clickbait in Feed." Facebook Newsroom, August 4, 2016. https://newsroom.fb.com/news/2016/08/news-feed-fyi-further-reducing-clickbait-in-feed.

Raloff, Janet. "Fact Checking: How to Think Like a Journalist." Science News for Students, September 21, 2017. https://www.sciencenewsforstudents.org/blog/outside-comment/fact-checking-how-think-journalist.

Silverman, Craig, and Lawrence Alexander. "How Teens in the Balkans Are Duping Trump Supporters with Fake News." *BuzzFeed News*, November 3, 2016. https://www.buzzfeed.com/craigsilverman/how-macedonia-became-a-global-hub-for-pro-trump-misinfo?utm_term=.woaPOArAB#.qjya8vPv4.

Smith, Brad. "Clickbait Copycat: How Can You Resist Clicking These 10 Facebook Ads? (Part 2)." AdEspresso, July 4, 2016. https://adespresso.com/blog/clickbait-facebook-advertising-examples.

Subramanian, Samanth. "Inside the Macedonian Fake-News Complex." *Wired*, February 15, 2017. https://www.wired.com/2017/02/veles-macedonia-fake-news.

Wu, Tim. "How the Media Came to Embrace Clickbait: An Internet History." KQED, May 12, 2017. https://www.kqed.org/futureofyou/387142.

INDEX

Page numbers in **boldface** are illustrations.

AdEspresso, 36–37, 39
ad tracking, 10, 17, 50
algorithm, 19
artificial intelligence, 24

bias, 41, 43–44, 48, 53
Burns, Evan, 49

circus, 6, **6**
Contagious Media
    Showdown, 12
critical thinking, 16, 20, 45,
    54
curiosity gap, 5–6, 21,
    30–31, 52
cute animal photos, 13,
    32–34, **33**, 36, 50

dopamine, 33–34, 36

Eidnes, Lars, 24, **24**
emotional manipulation,
    29–30, 39, 51
engaging headlines, 21

fabricate, 16
Facebook, 10, 17, 19, 26,
    35–36
fake news, 10, 16, **17**, 54
Federal Trade Commission,
    10
France, Adrian, 49

Hearst, William Randolph, 9
Huffington Post, 12, 26
Hughes, Jazmine, 7

influencer marketing, 10
infomercial, 8–9
information gap theory,
    30–31

landing page, 17
listicles, 31, 54
Loewenstein, George,
    30–31, **31**

Mays, Billy, **8**
monkey experiment, 33–34,
    36
Musetto, Vinnie, 9

native advertising, 39–40, 48

New York Journal, 9

New York Post, 9

New York World, 9

"9 Out of 10 Americans ..." article, 50–54, **51**

Odyssey, 49, **49**

page view, 18–19, 39

parasitic bird headline, 21, **21**

Peretti, Jonah, 12

PlayBuzz, 26

Pulitzer, Joseph, 9

reverse search, 38

robocalls, 37–38

Sapolsky, Robert, 33–34, 36

sensational, 9–10, 39

skeptical, 41

SMELL test, 42–45

Snopes, 10–11, **11**, 17

source, 35, 39–45, 47

Spartz, Emerson, 55

sponsored content, 39, 41, 48, **48**

Stanford Graduate School of Education study, 47–48

Trump, Donald, 23, 25–26, **26**

2016 presidential election, 23, 25

Upworthy, 50, 54

URL, 23, 25

Veles, Macedonia, 23, 25–27, **25**

verifiable, 22

viral content, 12, 15–16, 55

virologist, 55

Wright brothers, 22, **23**

yellow journalism, 9

ABOUT THE AUTHOR

Kristin Thiel lives in Portland, Oregon, where she is a writer and editor of books, articles, and documents for publishers, individuals, and businesses. She is the author of numerous books for young readers. Thiel was the lead writer on a report for her city about funding for high school dropout prevention. She has also judged YA book contests and managed before-school and afterschool literacy programs for AmeriCorps VISTA.